BUILDING A MINECRAFT® *City*

by Sarah Guthals, PhD

WILEY

BUILDING A MINECRAFT® CITY

Published by: **John Wiley & Sons, Inc.,** 111 River Street, Hoboken, NJ 07030-5774, www.wiley.com

Copyright © 2016 by John Wiley & Sons, Inc., Hoboken, New Jersey

Published simultaneously in Canada

No part of this publication may be reproduced, stored in a retrieval system or transmitted in any form or by any means, electronic, mechanical, photocopying, recording, scanning or otherwise, except as permitted under Sections 107 or 108 of the 1976 United States Copyright Act, without the prior written permission of the Publisher. Requests to the Publisher for permission should be addressed to the Permissions Department, John Wiley & Sons, Inc., 111 River Street, Hoboken, NJ 07030, (201) 748-6011, fax (201) 748-6008, or online at http://www.wiley.com/go/permissions.

Trademarks: Wiley, For Dummies, the Dummies Man logo, Dummies.com, Making Everything Easier, and related trade dress are trademarks or registered trademarks of John Wiley & Sons, Inc. and may not be used without written permission. Minecraft is a registered trademark of Mojang Synergies AB Corporation. All other trademarks are the property of their respective owners. John Wiley & Sons, Inc. is not associated with any product or vendor mentioned in this book.

For general information on our other products and services, please contact our Customer Care Department within the U.S. at 877-762-2974, outside the U.S. at 317-572-3993, or fax 317-572-4002. For technical support, please visit https://hub.wiley.com/community/support/dummies .

Wiley publishes in a variety of print and electronic formats and by print-on-demand. Some material included with standard print versions of this book may not be included in e-books or in print-on-demand. If this book refers to media such as a CD or DVD that is not included in the version you purchased, you may download this material at http://booksupport.wiley.com. For more information about Wiley products, visit www.wiley.com.

Library of Congress Control Number: 2016947915

ISBN 978-1-119-31641-1 (pbk); ISBN 978-1-119-31643-5 (ePub); 978-1-119-31645-9 (ePDF)

Manufactured in the United States of America

10 9 8 7 6 5 4 3 2 1

CONTENTS

PROJECT 3: BUILDING YOUR DREAM HOME   43

PROJECT 4: BUILDING YOUR OWN CITY   69

INTRODUCTION

SO YOU WANT TO LEARN HOW TO BUILD LIKE A PRO IN MINECRAFT? That's a great idea!

Building in Minecraft can be a ton of fun. Minecraft gives you an endless world to build, with infinite resources in Creative mode and a challenging resource collection in Survival mode. Whether you are on Minecraft PC or Minecraft PE, you can build homes, skyscrapers, fountains, and even water slides and roller coasters! This book gives you strategies for building and ideas for making an awesome Minecraft city that you and your friends will want to live and play in.

ABOUT MINECRAFT

Minecraft is a world made out of blocks. You can play in two modes: Creative and Survival.

In Creative mode, you have an infinite inventory of resources at your fingertips. You can fly and you never die. You can build anything you want to build, and you have a world that never ends to build it in.

In Survival mode, you have to live by the rules of the world. You have to find resources by breaking down trees to build tools to help you mine for metals and rocks. You use furnaces and crafting tables to turn raw materials into usable ones, and you have to defend yourself against creepers, skeletons, endermen, and spiders at night.

Either way you play, you will have fun and get to be in control of your very own world.

ABOUT THIS BOOK

Building a Minecraft City has four projects that help you learn how to create homes, skyscrapers, fountains, and city attractions like roller coasters. The earlier projects are simpler and easier to do in any version of Minecraft (PC or PE and Survival or Creative). Some of the later projects will work best on Minecraft PC in Creative mode.

Sometimes in this book you're asked to type commands. Commands will be in monofont. If you're reading this as an ebook, you can tap web addresses to visit websites, like this: www.dummies.com.

ABOUT YOU

Everybody has to start somewhere, right? I had to start writing this book by assuming that you're comfortable doing this stuff:

» **Typing on a computer and using a mouse or mobile device**. You may know how to use a Windows system or a Mac; either one will do. You might even be playing Minecraft on a mobile device, like an iPhone, iPad, or Android tablet. This book shows examples on a Mac and sometimes on an iPhone.

» **Playing Minecraft**. You don't need to be a Minecraft expert, and you don't have to be an expert Minecraft Builder. You can play on Windows or Mac for Minecraft PC and on any mobile device for Minecraft Pocket Edition (PE). Not everything in this book will work on Minecraft PE.

ABOUT THE ICONS

As you read through the projects in this book, you'll see a few icons. The icons point out different things:

Watch out! This icon comes with important information that may save you from the trouble that the pro builders sometimes have.

The Remember icon comes with ideas that you should keep in mind.

The Tip icon marks advice and shortcuts that can make building easier.

BEYOND THE BOOK

In addition to what you're reading right now, this product also comes with a free access-anywhere Cheat Sheet that gives you some pointers on building better Minecraft projects. To get this Cheat Sheet, simply go to www.dummies.com and search for "Building a Minecraft City Cheat Sheet" in the Search box.

PROJECT 1 ENTERING MINECRAFT

```
                    Create New World

    World Name

    Wiley's World

    Will be saved in: Wiley's World


                Game Mode: Survival
    Search for resources, crafting, gain
    levels, health and hunger


                More World Options...

    Create New World              Cancel
```

IN THE SANDBOX-SURVIVAL GAME OF MINECRAFT, YOU BUILD STRUCTURES, FIGHT MONSTERS, COLLECT ITEMS, MINE MINERALS, AND WORK TOWARD YOUR OWN GOALS. This 3-D, grid-based game features naturally generated landscapes and challenges.

In *Survival mode,* you must manage your resources and acquire increasingly useful items to advance through the game. In *Creative mode,* you can build or design whatever structure, setup, or invention you want in your personal universe. However, most of the information you need is found in Survival mode. This project explains how to obtain Minecraft, start on a Survival world, and familiarize yourself with the basic game controls.

REGISTERING A MINECRAFT ACCOUNT

To jump into the action, you first have to register a Minecraft account. Then you can play in Demo mode or upgrade to a Premium account, which you need for the full version. Follow these steps to register an account:

1 Go to http://minecraft.net.

The Minecraft home page opens.

2 Click on the Register link in the upper-right corner of the page.

The Register New Mojang Account page appears.

3 Fill out all the information requested in the text boxes, specify your date of birth, and answer the security questions.

4 Click on the Register button to finish.

5 Check the email account you entered for a verification message from Minecraft.

6 Click on the link provided in the email to complete your registration.

Check out the next section to find out how to purchase the game.

PURCHASING AND INSTALLING MINECRAFT

To buy and install the game, log in to your account at http://minecraft.net. (See the preceding section for details on registering.) Then follow these steps:

1 Click on the large Buy Now button on the home page.

The Minecraft Store page opens.

2 **Click on the Buy Minecraft for This Account option in the upper-left corner of the store.**

At the time of this writing, the cost of the game is $26.95.

If you can't click the button, you may not be logged in (or you may have already bought the game).

3 **Fill out your payment information and then click the Proceed to Checkout button.**

4 **Follow the necessary steps to complete your purchase.**

5 **Return to the Minecraft home page.**

On the right side of the screen, the large Buy Now button should now be labeled Download Now.

6 **Click on the Download Now button to open the Download page.**

7 **If you're using Windows, click to download and save the file anywhere on your computer.**

To view instructions for other operating systems, click the Show All Platforms button.

8 **Double-click the file to install the game.**

Your payment is immediately attributed to your account, so, if necessary, you can download the file again for free. The Minecraft home page also gives you the option to play from your browser — click the link under the Download Now button.

PLAYING THE GAME

After you install Minecraft, you're ready to start playing the game. To start, run the launcher you downloaded.

LOGGING IN AND OPERATING THE MAIN MENU

The launcher opens the news screen, which displays game updates and links. Enter your username and password in the lower-right corner and click Log In to continue to the main menu.

This list describes what you can do after you click the buttons on the main menu:

» **Singleplayer:** Start or continue a basic game. This project covers the options for starting a game in SinglePlayer mode.

» **Multiplayer:** Join other players online.

» **Languages:** Change the language of the text in Minecraft. This tiny button next to Options is indicated by a speech bubble containing a globe.

» **Options:** Manage game options such as sound, graphics, mouse controls, difficulty levels, and general settings.

» **Quit Game:** Close the window, unless you're in In-Browser mode.

STARTING YOUR FIRST GAME IN SINGLEPLAYER MODE

To start your first game in SinglePlayer mode, follow these steps:

1 **Click on the Singleplayer button to view a list of all your worlds.**

If you're just starting out in Minecraft, this list should be empty.

2 **Click on the Create New World button to start a new game.**

The world-creation page appears.

3 **In the World Name text box, type whatever name you want and click the Create New World button at the bottom.**

To turn on game cheats, special powers that provide a more casual experience, click the More World Options button, and then click the Allow Cheats button to turn cheats on or off. Cheats make the game stress-free when you're getting started by giving you more control over the world.

When you finish creating your world, the game automatically starts by generating the world and placing your *avatar* (character) in it.

UNDERSTANDING BASIC CONTROLS

The world of Minecraft is made of cubic *blocks*, materials such as dirt or stone that you can break down and rebuild into houses or craft into useful items. A block made of a material such as sand is referred to as a *sand block*. Because the side length of every block measures 1 meter, most distances are measured in blocks as well: If you read about an object that's located "three blocks up," it's the distance from the ground to the top of a stack of three blocks.

In addition to building and crafting, you have to defend against monsters and eventually face them head-on. As the game progresses, your goal becomes less about surviving and more about building structures, gathering resources, and facing challenges to gain access to more blocks and items.

To survive, you have to know how to move around, attack enemies, and manipulate the blocks that comprise the world. Table 1-1 lists the default key assignments for each control.

If you reassign any major keys, you may cause confusion later in the game.

Walk around and explore the world. After you get the hang of using the controls and you're prepared to immerse yourself in the fun and challenge of the real game, it's time to figure out how to survive.

TABLE 1-1 DEFAULT CONTROLS IN MINECRAFT

Action	Control	What Happens When You Use It
Pause	Esc	The game pauses (only in SinglePlayer mode), and the Game menu opens. Click Options ⇨ Controls to change the controls for certain actions. You can also close menus and other in-game screens.
Forward	W	Your avatar moves forward when this key is held down. Double-tapping the W key makes the character sprint — and makes the avatar hungry.
Back	S	Your avatar backs up.
Left	A	Your avatar moves to the left.
Right	D	Your avatar moves to the right.
Look	Mouse movement	Your avatar looks around. The Forward control always makes the avatar move in the direction you're looking.
Jump	Space	Your avatar jumps over one block at a time. Use this control while moving to make your way around rough terrain or jump over gaps. Jump while sprinting to leap over a great distance! Hold down this button while swimming to swim upward or to keep your avatar's head above water.

Action	Control	What Happens When You Use It
Attack	Left mouse button	Your character attacks in the direction of the crosshair in the middle of the screen. Tap the button to punch nearby entities, or hold down the button to break nearby blocks.
Use Item	Right mouse button	Your character uses the selected item.
Drop	Q	Your character drops the selected item.
Sneak	Left Shift	Your character moves slower, but cannot walk off edges. In MultiPlayer mode, other players can't see your avatar's name tag if a block is in the way.
Inventory	E	Your avatar's inventory is shown, and any open menus except the Pause menu are closed.
Chat	T	The Chat menu opens. Type a message, and then press Enter to talk to friends in multiplayer worlds or implement cheat commands.
List Players	L	A list of all players in the world is shown (disabled in single-player worlds).

(continued)

TABLE 1-1 (CONTINUED)

Action	Control	What Happens When You Use It
Pick Block	Middle mouse button	Click nearby blocks or entities with the middle mouse button to put them into the bottom row of your inventory, possibly replacing the selected item. It works only in Creative mode. If your mouse has no middle button, reassign this key on the Pause menu.
Command	/	The Chat menu opens and shows a slash mark (/), used for cheat commands.
Hide GUI	F1	All visual images are turned off, except for the player's view of the world (used for capturing imagery).
Screenshot	F2	A screenshot of the current view is taken.
View Performance	Shift+F3	(Rarely used.) You can view the game performance, and everything on the F3 menu.
View Statistics	F3	Your character's coordinates, current biome, and other information are shown. The y-axis points upward.
Change View	F5	The camera view changes between first-person view (recommended), third-person view, and in front of the avatar looking back at the avatar.
Smooth Movement	F8	This makes the mouse cursor move more smoothly (used for recording).

WATCHING THE HEADS-UP DISPLAY (HUD)

The little arrangement at the bottom of the screen is known as the Heads-Up Display, or HUD. To show the important details of your character, the HUD features these sections.

» **Health bar:** These ten hearts monitor the health of your avatar. As your avatar incurs damage, the hearts disappear. After all ten are depleted, your avatar dies and reappears at its *spawn point,* a position that can be changed by sleeping in a bed.

Your avatar can take damage by falling from ledges four blocks tall, colliding with harmful blocks or entities, or succumbing to other dangers such as drowning. When you equip yourself with armor, the Armor bar appears over the Health bar, indicating the protective value of your armor.

» **Inventory:** These nine squares contain items you've collected, and they're the only squares in the inventory that you can access without pressing E. You can use the 1–9 keys or the scroll wheel to select items, and right-click to use them. If you're using a sword or a tool for breaking blocks faster (such as an axe), the item will automatically function when you left-click on it.

» **Experience**: The green Experience bar fills up when you collect *experience orbs.* These orbs appear naturally whenever you defeat monsters, smelt items in a furnace, breed animals, or mine any ore except iron or gold. When the bar is full, a number appears or increases over it, indicating your experience level. You can spend levels with anvils or enchantment tables, but you will lose them if you die.

» **Hunger bar:** This bar represents your food supply. The emptier the bar, the hungrier you are.

» **Breath:** When your avatar's head goes underwater, ten bubbles appear just above your Hunger bar and begin to pop one by one. This signifies how long you can hold your breath; if all the bubbles are gone and you're still underwater, your Health bar begins to deplete.

Carefully monitor the Health and Hunger bars, and organize your inventory slots for easy access.

PROJECT 2 PREBUILDING STRATEGIES

IN THIS PROJECT, YOU LEARN HOW TO GATHER AND ORGANIZE ALL THE MATERIALS YOU'LL NEED TO BUILD. You also get tips on how to find the perfect landscape for your buildings and outline what you plan on building.

In Minecraft, you can build all kinds of different structures in many interesting environments. The basic concepts are simple (gather blocks and stack them), but you need a lot of practice to master building. Sometimes it is hard to figure out *what* you want to build, which materials you need, how big the building should be, and how to build it. This project shows you how to prepare for building.

BUILDING DIFFERENT MINECRAFT BUILDINGS

You can build lots of items using the blocks available to you in Minecraft. Here are just a few of the options:

» **Shacks and shelters:** Simple shelter for surviving the night.

» **Houses and mansions:** A bigger shelter for living in.

» **Castles:** A huge castle with moats and bridges.

» **Underground hideouts:** An underground shelter attached to mines.

» **Functional buildings:** Automatic farming and elevators.

» **Villages and cities**: Areas of your Minecraft world that include all of these structures.

With enough practice, you can design any of these sorts of buildings — and whatever else you can think of.

If you're not sure what you'd like to build, see the nearby sidebar "So, what do you want to build?"

SO, WHAT DO YOU WANT TO BUILD?

The first step to building a large-scale build is figuring out exactly what it is that you want to create. What's the building's purpose? What type of build is it? Is it large or small? What color should it be?

First, focus on the purpose of the building. How do you want to use it? Is it only for decoration, or does it have a function? For example, a library is for decoration, whereas a house serves a specific need. If your building is for decoration only, you don't have to think much about the purpose — you can focus on how the building will look. If your building has a specific function, think more about what you need to build or place inside and out (such as a furnace or a place to mine). Though your building should look nice, the decorative aspect is secondary.

Where you decide to build contributes to your building's look. If you're building a library in the middle of a city, look at other structures in the city. For example, are they all square, or are they rounded? If all other structures are square, your library should be square, too — if it were rounded, it would look out of place. If you notice any other characteristics that the existing buildings have (such as a certain style of roof or a repeating color), use that same element in your building also so that it all fits together.

If you're unsure about which color best suits your building, consider its purpose (is it decorative or functional?), but also think about how you want it to look. For example, if you want your castle to look old and abandoned, use gray, cracked blocks, like cobblestone or moss stone, to build. If you want your building to look new and modern, use iron blocks or glowstone instead.

GATHERING MATERIALS FOR CONSTRUCTION: CREATIVE MODE

Every building is made out of blocks. Putting the blocks that you will use into your inventory will make designing and building much faster.

There are two ways to play Minecraft: Creative mode and Survival mode. Playing in Creative mode allows you to use every block without having to search the world for it and can help you understand what you can use in future projects that you want to build in Survival mode. You can play in Creative mode on both the PC and PE version of Minecraft!

SETTING UP THE INVENTORY IN CREATIVE MODE

When building in Creative mode, you can add any item you want to the inventory. The first step is to decide on the materials you want to build your structure with. For this first project, maybe you want to use wood, brick, and glass. You can use different types of wood, brick, and glass blocks, too. For example, you may want to grab the block and stair version of the wood and brick and the block and pane version of the glass. You can also grab the ladder and fence items so that you can stake out your yard and get ready for multiple stories.

It is always a good idea to grab a block of dirt so that you can replace any blocks you accidentally break.

USING THE CREATIVE MODE MENU

To open your Inventory menu, all you have to do is press the letter *e* on your keyboard — the default key, in other words. On your PC, you will see 12 tabs.

This book will focus on Minecraft PC Version, Creative mode, but throughout the book, you will find tips for what to do in Survival mode or Minecraft PE.

On your Pocket Edition, you should press the inventory button at the right of your inventory to open your inventory menu. When you press the inventory button, you will see seven tabs.

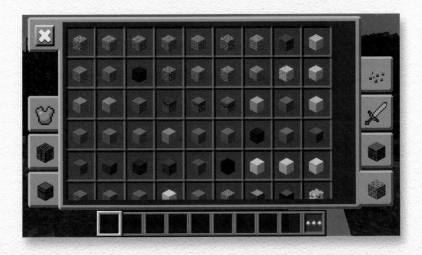

In Survival mode, you won't have any tabs on Minecraft PC.

And you will only have three tabs on Minecraft PE.

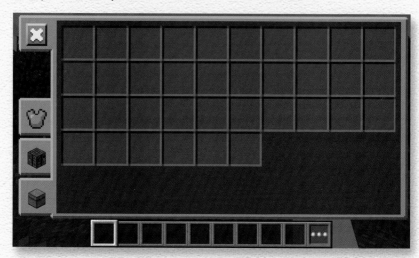

In Minecraft PC Creative mode, you can scroll through the blocks using either the scroll wheel or the slider on the right side of the menu.

If you don't want to spend a lot of time looking for the item you want, the menu is surrounded by 12 clickable tabs that you can use to narrow your search and complete projects much faster. This list describes the tabs:

» **Building Blocks:** The tab in the upper-left corner, represented by the Bricks icon, contains 150 different types of blocks.

» **Decoration Blocks:** This tab, represented by peonies (a type of flower), has decorations like flowers.

» **Redstone:** Represented by a lump of redstone dust, this tab has everything you need to make functional structures.

» **Transportation**: This small section, which a booster rail represents, has transportation items, like minecarts.

» **Miscellaneous:** Represented by a lava bucket, this tab has a ton of miscellaneous items like buckets of water.

» **Foodstuffs, Tools, Combat, Brewing, and Materials:** The five tabs at the lower-left contain food items, tools, weapons, potions, and crafting materials.

» **Search Items**: This section (not really a tab, I admit) is represented by the Compass icon, which actually works, even on the Inventory menu. This tab lets you search for items. Try it! Type in "Brick" and you will see everything brick-related!

» **Survival Inventory:** Represented by a chest in the lower-right corner of the Menu screen, this tab shows a screen that looks more like the Survival mode inventory.

If you hold down the Shift key before clicking on an item on the Creative mode menu, you get a full stack of those items — the largest number that can fit in a single inventory slot. For example, if you Shift + click on a dirt block on this menu, you pick up 64 of those dirt blocks.

You can pick up an item, click on a different tab, and then place the item. You can then easily bring an item from the Creative mode menu into any slot of the inventory.

ORGANIZING YOUR MATERIALS FOR SURVIVAL MODE

Sometimes you want to build in Creative mode, but then switch to Survival mode after you have finished building to play with the creatures and defend yourself throughout the nights.

If you want to switch between Creative and Survival mode on either the PC or PE edition, you may want to make sure that you are bringing all the supplies with you that you will need.

In Survival mode, as you can see in the next section, you do not have access to unlimited inventory. But you can strategically place chests, crafting tables, and furnaces around your building. Then you can stockpile your chests with lots of blocks and items that you will need once you switch to Survival mode.

A good trick is to place two chests right next to each other, which will make a chest that is twice as big. This makes it faster to find items, because you can store more items in one larger chest.

OBTAINING A GOOD INVENTORY IN SURVIVAL MODE

It's harder to obtain tools in Survival mode than it is in Creative mode, mostly because of these issues:

» **You have to find all the items you need to use.** Unlike in Creative mode, there's no handy menu where you can go to get them.

» **Most items you use leave the inventory.** If you need more of something, you have to make or find more of it. When you use items like arrows or seeds in Creative mode, they don't leave your inventory.

» **You can't break blocks instantly.** It's a bummer because some blocks take a long time to break, and they require tools if you want to break them quickly. And certain blocks (such as smooth stone) don't return the same item to the inventory when you destroy them.

» **You can't fly.** Unfortunately, flight is a luxury reserved for Creative mode. You have to get creative if you need to reach tall places.

What all this means is that in Survival mode, you need to have a lot more items on hand than you do in Creative mode. For example, if you're going to use quite a bit of a particular block in a project, you should gather a lot of those blocks in the inventory before you start.

To give you an idea of what I'm talking about, this is the inventory of someone who is about to start building in Survival mode.

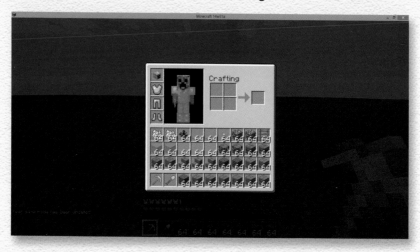

For any large-scale building project, bring these items with you when you start:

» **Tools:** In case you need to destroy a block for whatever reason, bringing tools with you saves a few resources and a ton of time. The tools you bring depend on the sort of blocks you're working with:

   » *Pickaxes* help destroy stone- and metal-based blocks.

   » *Axes* are good at destroying wooden blocks.

   » *Shovels* are best against soft blocks, such as dirt, sand, or gravel.

» **The main blocks you want to build with:** These can be just about anything, though most players have wooden planks, cobblestone, or the like. (If you're not sure which blocks you need, see the nearby sidebar "Selecting blocks.")

SELECTING BLOCKS

Choosing blocks is simple: Just refer to your original plans and pick the type of block that matches the idea. For example, if you want your building to look ancient or abandoned, use cracked blocks that look like cracked stone bricks. If you want your building to look colorful and lively, use dyed wool.

If you didn't plan out the color of your building first, don't worry — doing so is easy. If you created the building with a specific theme, pick the color of the blocks based on that theme. If you built your structure to resemble a library instead, consider using bookshelves for the exterior blocks. If you're building a museum and you want it to look fancy on the outside, you can choose a block with a silver or tan color. For a more modern feel, on the other hand, choose blocks with a color that stands out, such as glowstone (gold) or purple wool (for purple).

As always, keep an eye on the surroundings of your new building. Most of the time, the new structure should blend in with its surroundings rather than stick out like a sore thumb. If you're in an evergreen forest, for example, a wooden plank house would fit in, but a sandstone house wouldn't, because that particular tan doesn't quite mesh with the greens and browns of the woods.

» **Any decoration blocks that you want to place immediately:** You can place decorations as you build, but I suggest saving them until after you complete the general structure of the building.

» **Other necessary items:** For example, the inventory shown in the previous figure includes bonemeal, which you need if you want to grow various plants (including saplings, which are also in the player's inventory).

Always gather more materials than you need. If you acquire too much, you can save the leftovers for future projects. If you acquire too little, you have to go all the way back in order to gather more.

In Survival mode or Creative mode, put your most commonly used items in the first four slots of the bottom row of the inventory. The keys to access these slots are much easier to reach, because the 1 to 4 keys are closer to the default movement keys. You can also use the scroll wheel to select different objects in your hot-bar, and it's easier to do that if similar items are grouped close together.

ORGANIZING YOUR MATERIALS IN SURVIVAL MODE

When you start a build, it's a good idea to gather all your materials in one place. Going back and forth between gathering, crafting, and building is a pain. It's a lot easier if everything is in the same place before you start. To organize your materials, follow these steps:

1 Figure out what materials you want to gather and make.

2 Set up chests and crafting stations.

Before you start on a project, it's a good idea to set up a few chests and crafting tables. This will make it so that a) you don't have to run back and forth to get items and b) you have quick access to things like furnaces.

3 **Gather all the raw materials you need.**

You should have a handy list ready if you did Step 1, so set off and gather those materials!

4 **Craft all the other materials you need.**

5 **Sort your resources into different chests so that you know where to find things quickly.**

GETTING READY TO BUILD IN PORTABLE EDITION

In Minecraft Portable Edition, there are very similar rules that apply in both Creative mode and Survival mode as described in the preceding sections. However, there are some differences with the inventory options and how the crafting happens.

One of the biggest differences is that when you are in Survival mode on Minecraft PE, you don't have to remember the crafting recipes. For example, you can see that a lot of different kinds of wood are in the lower inventory. When the crafting table is opened, Minecraft PE gives you everything that you can build; all you have to do is choose the item from the left side and click on the button on the right side underneath the crafting area.

GETTING AROUND THE STRUCTURE

In Creative mode, you can fly and move quickly around buildings. In Survival mode, you can't, meaning you have to come up with ways to move around. In Survival mode, you sometimes have to get creative with how you navigate the build.

USING SCAFFOLDING

If you need to build in hard-to-reach areas, you can use *scaffolding*. In other words, you can build a pillar of blocks as high as you need so that you can build items such as roofs and tall towers. To use scaffolding, follow these steps:

1 **Get some easy-to-break blocks, like dirt or sand blocks.**

2 **Using the mouse, "look" straight down while standing next to the place you want to climb up to.**

3 **Hold down the the right button on your mouse.**

   You're building a pillar that raises you up so that you can work.

4 **Continue looking down and repeating Step 3 until you're as high as you need to be to work.**

5 **To then place blocks horizontally at your new level, press the Shift key so that you can crawl to the very edge of the blocks and then place a block there.**

6 **Continue placing blocks horizontally until you've reached where you need to be to continue building.**

7 **When you're done with your work, stand on the pillar of blocks you've built, look down, and hold the left button on your mouse.**

You're destroying all the blocks in the pillar so that you can get down to the ground.

This is what a scaffold might look like:

Sand and gravel make good scaffolding because they're easy to destroy. If you destroy the bottom block of a sand or gravel pillar and then quickly replace it with a torch or another nonsolid block, the pillar collapses into a pile of sand or gravel items for you.

USING LADDERS TO SCALE YOUR STRUCTURE

Ladders are cheap, and they help you climb walls quickly. Just follow these steps to use a ladder on your building:

1 **Walk up to the wall and put the ladder in your hot bar either by pressing the corresponding number or by navigating to it with the scroll wheel.**

2 **Press and hold the right button on your mouse.**

3 **Keep your eye on the wall and hold the Forward key (W, by default) to climb the ladder.**

   As you climb, you can place more ladders in front of you by holding down the right mouse button.

Your stairs might look like this:

LOCATION IS EVERYTHING

Before you start building, you need to figure out where to build. Plains and deserts generally make for usable, flat building ground, but what if you want to build your structure on a mountain? Or what if you can't find a flat area that's large enough to build a mansion? Not sure where to build? See the nearby sidebar "Where do you want to be?" for some tips.

WHERE DO YOU WANT TO BE?

Setting up the area before you start building is a huge help — that little bit of prep work can often let you know whether you have enough room to build — and it can help you keep on track as you build.

To set up the area, you first need to *find* an area. Where do you want to be? On the beach? In the woods? In a city? But don't forget about the type of build you're starting — that aspect makes a difference in where you build. For example, a hospital in the middle of the woods doesn't look quite right. It makes more sense to place a hospital in a city.

After you find an area you like, start clearing it — you need an open space to build in. To clear an area, destroy any trees, grass, or flowers that are in your way. (To destroy blocks, left click the mouse button.)

As you clear the area, look to see whether you can spot any water or lava near you. If you do, find out where it's coming from, and try to stop the flow. The only reason that water might be helpful to you is if you want to build a farm. Other than that, the water will most likely just get in your way. If the water or lava is coming from a single hole in a mountain wall, place a single block in that hole to stop the flow.

Always ensure that your surroundings are safe — the last thing you want is to accidentally fall into a lava pool, for example.

BUILDING ON FUN LANDSCAPES

The great thing about Minecraft is that every single world that you enter already has thousands of blocks placed for you, so you may want to build your structure using the blocks that are already there. Like this mountain town:

If you want to create a building on an existing natural structure, follow these steps:

1 **Decide how much of the building can fit inside the natural structure.**

If you want to build on a mountain, see how much you can put in or around the mountain. Or, if you want to build in a cave, decide how much of the structure should fit inside the cave.

The structure isn't limited to the mountain or cave — you're simply deciding where to start. You can change things later.

2 **Dig out the space to make way for your buildings.**

3 Construct any large buildings that tie together the theme of the structure — like bridges!

4 Create the rest of your buildings.

While you work, step back every once in a while to make sure that the buildings still fit in with the landscape.

5 Decorate the interiors of your buildings.

RESHAPING THE LANDSCAPE

Though landscapes allow for lots of neat-looking creations, sometimes the landscape you have isn't quite the one you want. Fortunately, you can change the world however you want; it just takes some time.

A common problem when building is finding flat ground to build on. Even a flat area isn't always 100 percent flat:

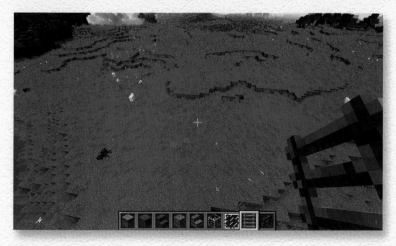

LEVELING MOSTLY FLAT SURFACES

If a surface has a few bumps and dips, you can make it completely flat by following these steps:

1 **Get the largest piece of flat land you can find.**

2 **Destroy any small hills inside the land.**

3 **Fill any holes in the land.**

4 **Level other hills and holes at the edge of the land, extending the land until it's big enough to support your building.**

LEVELING LARGE STRUCTURES

Sometimes you want even more room to build a structure. You might destroy an entire hill to make way for your building, for example, or hollow out a mountain to build an underground home.

Some players dig out these structures by hand, but you can use another method to clear out land: TNT.

To mine out large areas with TNT, you can follow one of two different methods:

» Maintain a distance of at least three to five blocks between each block of TNT you use. This method is the safer one. When you spread out explosives this way, you can carve out holes in any shape you want, hollowing out caves or reducing hills to flatter surfaces.

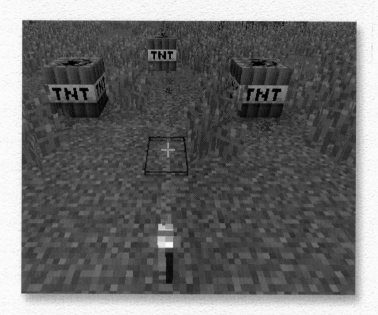

» Place a cluster of TNT (for example, a 3 x 3 x 3 cube) at the center of the place you want to destroy. This method is riskier and inaccurate, but it's easier to complete.

When TNT is in close quarters like this, some of the explosives tend to launch off-course and can destroy other structures (even those you want to keep).

 You can light TNT in lots of simple ways after you place it. You can use pressure plates, redstone torches, flint and steel, bows with the Flame enchantment, and many other tools. None of these methods changes the way the TNT detonates, so use whichever one is most convenient.

WIRE FRAMING THE BUILD ON PAPER

After your landscape is how you want it, you will want to build an outline of your building first — also called a *wire frame*.

Before building your wire frame in Minecraft, you may want to draw it out on paper first — maybe use graph paper — or use some kind of blocks that you might have.

 Designing and planning your building outside of the Minecraft environment first can help you avoid problems like miscalculating and needing to tear it all down, or running out of materials if you are in Survival mode.

To design your building on paper first, follow these steps:

1 **Count the size of your land.**

2 **Sketch the outer walls.**

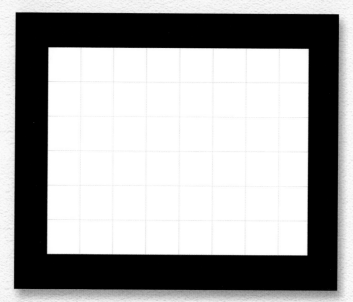

You don't have to have four walls. You can also have an interestingly shaped building.

3 **Sketch the inner walls, doors, and windows.**

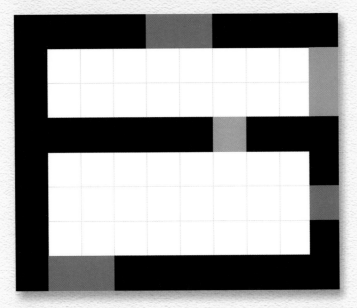

4 **Draw your furniture.**

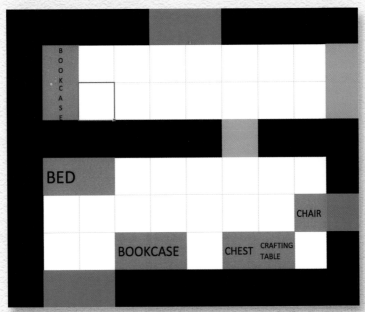

Don't be afraid to redo the design if you end up not liking it. That's why you did it on paper first!

WIRE FRAMING THE BUILD IN MINECRAFT

A wire frame is a temporary outline of a building — kind of a sample building — made of easy-to-break blocks, like dirt. Wire frames are handy because they help you see whether your original plan needs a tweak or two and let you estimate how many blocks you need for the final build.

After you have a drawn out wire frame on paper, it should be simple to build your wire frame in Minecraft.

Just like a real architect, when you get into your Minecraft world, new problems may arise, so you should still take some time to explore building your wire frame in Minecraft before building the entire structure.

A wire frame helps you see how your building will look with different floor plans and features. If you decide that you don't like a particular look, you can easily change it by breaking down a section and moving blocks around until you come up with a design you like.

The layout of your building is important. If you don't like it now and you decide to change it later, you may run into problems. Now is a good time to experiment with curves, varying floor and wall heights, ceilings, and roofs.

1 Using dirt blocks, outline the base of the structure.

This is an example of a wire frame that was built and then changed:

2 Using more dirt blocks, outline the structure's walls.

This step helps you estimate how high the walls should be. If you thought you wanted the walls to be five blocks high but the wire frame shows that it looks better with seven blocks, you can make a note of it when you're building the structure:

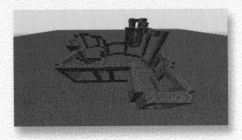

3 Revise, if needed.

After the floor and walls are outlined, you should have a good idea of what the structure will look like. While the structure is still easy to edit, go back and change anything that doesn't look right.

Don't forget the extras. Go ahead and wire frame anything you want to include in and around the building, such as fences and paths. Be sure to make good use of your wire frame when referencing your project when you actually start building your structure.

PROJECT 3 BUILDING YOUR DREAM HOME

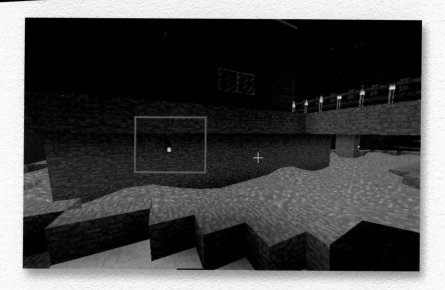

IN THIS PROJECT, YOU LEARN HOW TO BUILD YOUR ULTIMATE DREAM HOME. You also get tips on decorating your home and even protecting it from monsters in the night!

BUILDING YOUR FIRST BUILDING

The first step to mastering building is to make a simple structure to survive the night. The techniques you learn when building a simple survival structure can help you when you go on to build castles, cities, skyscrapers, and anything else that you can imagine.

CLEARING YOUR BUILDING SITE

In Project 2, you can find tips for finding the right site, but for this simple structure, just find a flat area. Make sure it's at least ten blocks wide and ten blocks long. You may have to break or add blocks to make it flat.

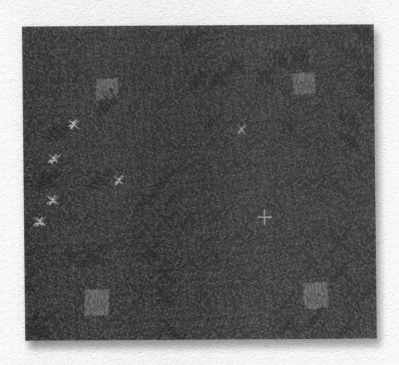

CHOOSING YOUR MATERIALS

In Project 2, you learn about setting up your inventory and get tips for using Creative mode and Survival mode. For your simple structure, you can use wood planks.

It's a good idea to keep a block of dirt or grass in your inventory, too. That way, if you accidentally break a block on the ground that you're building on, you can quickly replace it.

 If you are in Survival mode on Minecraft PC or Minecraft PE, then you will have to cut down trees before you get wood planks. Punch the tree trucks until they break. Collect at least ten wood blocks, press e (or the inventory button if you are on Minecraft PE), and put all your wood into the crafting area. Each piece of wood will give you four wooden planks!

Not sure which room to build first? See the nearby sidebar "Starting with a Central Room."

STARTING WITH A CENTRAL ROOM

After the area is cleared out and safe, it's time to start building! The best place to start is to build a central room, to serve as the hub of your build. It's the first room you enter, and you build all other rooms around it.

Building a central room is just like building any other room. First plan out the central room. Though this step may seem boring, don't skip it! Planning is vital because all the other rooms you build depend on the central room. If you build it and it's too large, you might run out of space quickly, and the other rooms you planned won't fit.

To determine the size of the central room, look at its original plans. How big are the other rooms supposed to be? How much room does that leave for your central room?

BUILDING WALLS

After you choose your materials, you're ready to build your four walls. Later you can build other structures with a different number of walls, but for this first structure, just building four walls is important.

1 Use the wood planks to make the outline of your simple structure.

2 Stack blocks on top of the wire frame until the wall is finished.

Make your walls at least three blocks tall so that you add a ceiling and still fit inside of your simple structure.

3 Continue building walls until you have made all four.

When you are placing each block, you can put the <+> on the side of a block you have already placed, instead of on the ground, and walk backwards. This makes placing blocks in a straight line a lot easier and faster.

BUILDING A CEILING

If you made your walls three blocks tall, then you should be able to put the + on the side of one of the top blocks and start filling in a ceiling.

If you made your walls very tall, and you can't put blocks on the sides, then you can build a simple scaffold out of dirt to reach the top.

As you're building your ceiling, make sure that you leave at least one block open so that you can see!

BUILDING A DOOR

The easiest door is a hole in a wall that is big enough for you to walk through.

But you may want to put an actual door so that monsters can't come in your house when it gets to be night. If you are in Creative mode, you can choose from any door you want.

If you are in Survival mode on Minecraft PC, then you should first make a crafting table by putting four wooden planks in a square in the crafting area of your inventory.

Then put the crafting table in your simple shelter and open it up by right-clicking on it. Put six wood planks in two columns to make a door.

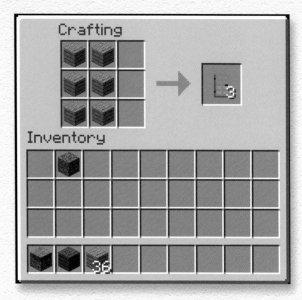

If you are in Survival mode on Minecraft PE, then you do the same steps, except your crafting area will tell you how to build a crafting table.

And your crafting table will tell you how to build your door.

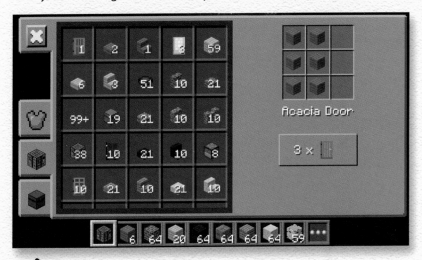

 Just make sure that you have enough wood planks. If you don't, go chop down some more trees!

Now that you have a door, you have a functional simple structure!

ADDING LIGHT

You can add light to your home in three ways:

» Create a skylight.

» Make windows.

» Add torches.

If you ever need to know how to craft something in Survival mode, you can go onto the Internet with your parent's permission and look it up. For example, http://minecraft-crafting.net is a great resource!

BUILDING YOUR DREAM HOME

After you have your basic building skills, you can build your dream home. To start, you have several options:

» **Start from scratch.** Find a new area and make a new wire frame.

» **Start from your simple structure.** Just because it started as a simple structure doesn't mean you can turn it into a dream house.

» **Start from your wire frame from Project 2.** If you did a creative wire frame in Project 2, you can start from there.

In Project 2, you learn that drawing your wire frame is a great way to start. Starting from a drawing, you can build your dream house with these steps:

1 Draw your wire frame.

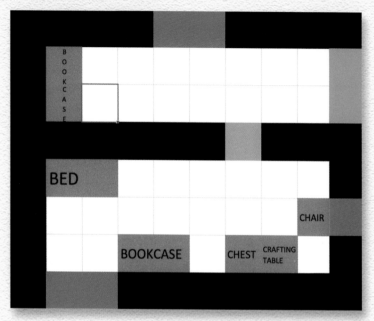

2 Clear your landscape.

3 **Make your wire frame in Minecraft.**

4 **Add your walls and ceiling.**

TIP

Consider making your ceiling 3D instead of just flat!

5 **Put in your doors and windows.**

6 Add your interior decorations.

You can get a frame from the inventory and then put an item in the frame by holding the item in your hand and right-clicking with the mouse on the frame.

After you have built your dream home, you can always switch to Survival mode.

On Minecraft PC, just type

```
/gamemode s
```

On Minecraft PE, just pause the game by clicking the Pause button in the upper-right corner, and then click on the Quit to Title button. Once you are at the title screen, click on the pencil next to your world:

Click on Survival and then click on Back:

Then you can go into the world in Survival mode, but your house and everything in your chest will still be there.

ADDING A PERSONAL TOUCH

It's time for a tour! Enter your building and take a look around. It's pretty plain, right? Well, then, let's show you how to change the situation by decorating and adding some cool features.

If you have a theme in mind for your building or a specific purpose for it, start by adding items that fit your intentions. For example, if you built a house to live in, it needs some basic items, such as a furnace and a crafting table.

A house also needs light. A torch is a helpful light source, but you have other options, too. Glowstone not only looks good but also gives off a good amount of light. You can use redstone lamps, too. Or you can go with windows for natural light. If you truly want to get creative, build a glass ceiling — you'll always know what the weather's like!

Don't get too caught up in matching purpose and decorations. Just because your building has a purpose doesn't mean that you can't have fun items inside — it's okay to get creative. If you're decorating your house, for example, you can build bookcases, paintings, or stained glass items to add interest.

Later on, if you decide that you want to change the color of a wall or the decorations in your room, go ahead! Nothing is set in stone.

Try some of these to make your home more interesting:

» Use colored glass on your windows.

» Make a wall of all colored glass to let in a lot of light.

» Use colored wool to "paint" your walls.

» Make a basement by digging down in your home.

» Add a second story or attic with ladders or staircases.

» Make bunk beds.

» Make colorful lights using colored glass.

Be creative and don't be afraid to experiment!

PROTECTING YOUR DREAM HOME

After you have built and decorated your dream home, you can start protecting it.

One of the easiest ways to protect your home is to make surrounding protection, like fences or moats:

» Make a large platform in front of your house.

» Make a small platform all around your house.

» Dig a moat below your house and put lava in the moat.

» Put torches around your entire platform.

» Put fences around your entire front platform.

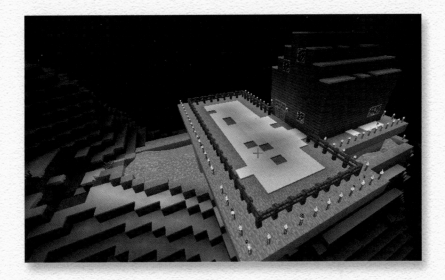

Now it will be hard for anyone to even come on your platform, and you will be able to see your house, even at night.

Lava can catch your house on fire if your house is made out of wood, so make sure that your lava (and the sparks it throws in the air) can't reach your house!

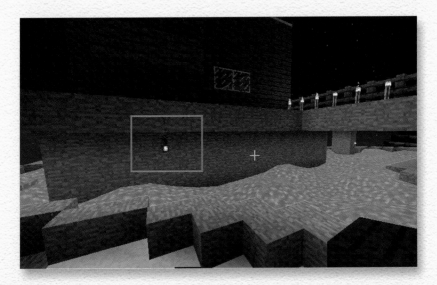

DON'T FORGET THE DETAILS

You have the outside finished. You have the inside finished. Now it's time to pay attention to the details. Elements such as trim, decorated doorways, and 3D designs can add pizazz to your build.

Trim makes the colors in your house stand out and helps your house look more three-dimensional (like a real-life house). Trim is all about the color of the blocks. Pick trim colors that complement each other. For example, wooden planks and nether brick go together well.

You can make the doorway stand out by adding some trim. Some people like to make their doors the same color as the trim, but you don't have to. The idea is to make sure that the door doesn't simply blend in with the wall.

THINKING ABOUT NEW DESIGNS

After you have built your first protected home, start thinking about new designs you want to make. In Project 4, you learn how to build an entire city. This city will have a lot of different kinds of buildings, and you learn how to copy and paste structures.

TWEAKING YOUR BUILDING CONSTANTLY

Congratulations! You're pretty much finished with your building. Now you have only one last step to complete and that's to never stop making your building better. If you decide one day that you want more windows, go ahead and build more windows. Don't be afraid to make changes — you can always change them back if your revision doesn't work out, or you can make additional changes to make your building better.

Go outside and look at your building. It's looking pretty cool, right? Even if it's looking good, you may see a component that looks somewhat odd or a place that needs sprucing up. No problem. If you see something you want to change, whether it's a major revision or a small tweak, go ahead and change it. That's the beauty of Minecraft — you can change anything at any time.

Be sure to look at your windows to see whether they match. Are they the same height? Are they the same number of blocks from each other? If not, and you want them to be more uniform, move them!

Another detail to examine is the door (or doors). At least once, we've built an item with a single door only to decide that I wanted a bigger one — so I built one. You can do this, too, by adding another door beside your first

(continued)

(continued)

one. When you do, the handles turn toward each other on their own.

When you're happy with the exterior details, take a look inside to see whether you want to change anything. If you do, go ahead and change it. This is your building, so it should look how you want it to look.

One element that players sometimes want to change is the flooring. You can use just about anything for the floor. You can make a lava or water floor. (Either one is cool!) But even block floors can be amazing — it all depends on the type of block you choose. Pick an interesting block such as nether brick or glowstone to make the floor look good. You can even add a pattern to the floor.

PROJECT 4 BUILDING YOUR OWN CITY

BUILDING HOUSES, HUTS, MANSIONS, AND CASTLES CAN BE FUN, BUT MAKING AN ENTIRE CITY IS WHERE YOU CAN REALLY SHOW OFF YOUR DESIGN SKILLS AND CREATE A PLACE FOR YOU AND YOUR FRIENDS TO PLAY IN YOUR MINECRAFT WORLD.

Building a city can be hard work and can take a really long time. One way to build a city faster is to team up with some of your friends. Have each person build a part of the city and then connect the different parts with paths, tunnels, or bridges.

PLANNING YOUR CITY

Planning your city is an important part of building a city because it saves your time later. If you don't plan, you may have to tear down and rebuild things, and your city won't look organized.

CHOOSING A THEME FOR YOUR CITY

Before you begin, make sure that you have some kind of inspiration for the kind of city you are going to build. Will this be a modern day city like New York? Or maybe an ancient city like Greece? Will this city have futuristic designs with building in the air? Or maybe you want to make a city that looks like you are on Mars!

Take a look at what other people have built to get your inspiration. With your parents, maybe go online to see what is possible. Or get together with your friends and imagine cities that you all love.

Cities that you build in Minecraft don't have to follow any certain rules. Maybe you want to build a sports-themed city with basketball courts everywhere and baseball fields at the end of each corner!

SKETCHING YOUR CITY

Just like planning to build a house, you can use paper and pencil to plan for your city. Your sketch should include paths, bridges, walls, and buildings.

Use different colors to mean different kinds of things in your city. For example, blue means path, while green means tunnel.

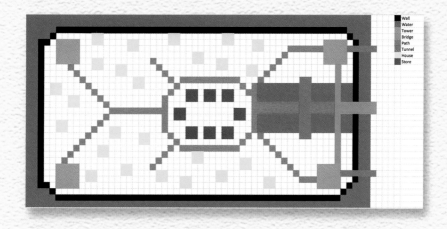

MAKING SPACE IN MINECRAFT

First you need to decide whether you want to have a city in a more natural Minecraft world or make it easier to build and have a city in a flat world.

NATURAL WORLD CITY

In a natural Minecraft world, you have a few options:

» **Make a mountain city.** Instead of getting rid of the mountains, you can just build a mountain city with houses as caves or houses hanging off the cliffs with bridges and paths connecting them all.

» **Find flatter areas.** In a more natural world, you can try to find flatter areas and tear down mountains with TNT or just by hand.

» **Build in the sky.** Another fun option is to build your city in the sky. Make floating platforms and bridges that connect them.

» **Make an underwater city.** A fun type of city is an underwater city; start by building a tunnel into the water and then make huge enclosures with lamps all around.

FLAT WORLD CITY

Another option is to create a flat world in Minecraft. When you are first making your world on Minecraft, you can choose to have a superflat world. This type of world will work on Minecraft PC and Minecraft PE and for Survival or Creative mode.

On Minecraft PC, you can name your world, choose Survival or Creative, and then click on More World Options.

```
                    Create New World

        World Name

        New World

        Will be saved in: New World-


                  Game Mode: Survival
        Search for resources, crafting, gain
        levels, health and hunger


                  More World Options...
        Create New World              Cancel
```

Then you can click on World Type until it says Superflat.

```
                    Create New World

         Seed for the World Generator


        Leave blank for a random seed

    Generate Structures: ON      World Type: Superflat
    Villages, dungeons etc              Customize

      Allow Cheats: OFF           Bonus Chest: OFF
    Commands like /gamemode, /xp
                        Done
        Create New World              Cancel
```

On Minecraft PE, you can name your world, choose Survival or Creative, and then click on Advanced.

Then you can click on Flat.

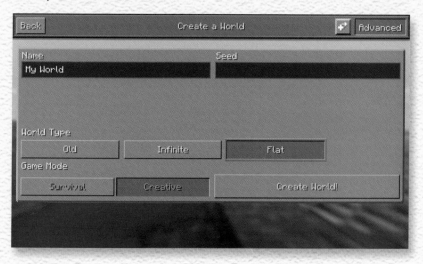

Starting with a flat world can make building the city you want easier, but it won't have a lot of interesting things like mountains. Don't worry, though; you can always build your own mountains!

 If you decide to use a flat world, don't dig too deep, or you will fall through the bottom of the world and die — even in Creative mode!

OUTLINING YOUR CITY

After you choose an area for your city, you're ready to outline it.

Start with the outer part of your city. If you want to have a wall around your city, build that first. If you want to have a path around your city, build that. If you don't want to have anything surrounding your city, maybe you can just put a temporary wall that is one block high so that you know where your city boundaries are.

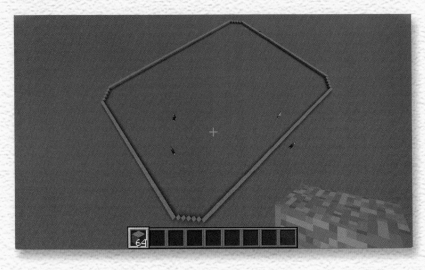

If you start your flat world and slimes are everywhere, you can always set the difficulty mode to peaceful. Just type

```
/difficult peaceful
```

and they will go away!

CONNECTING THE PATHS

Next, you should put in your paths, tunnels, and bridges — anything that you can build without the buildings. That way, you have a clear outline of your entire city.

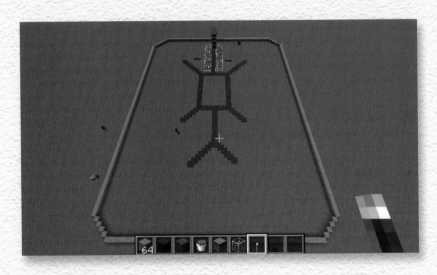

When you are making tunnels, be careful that you do not dig so deep that you fall through the ground. Even if you're in Creative mode, you will die! So dig down slowly and in front of you instead of underneath you.

STARTING CONSTRUCTION

Next, you can start building buildings. The fastest way to build a city is to make a couple buildings and then replicate them. This will make your city big, really fast.

After you finish making the buildings, you can make each one look a little different so that they don't all look exactly the same.

BUILDING A TALL BUILDING

Maybe you want to build a skyscraper or a tower. Whatever your tall building is, you may want to build something really tall, and doing it by hand can take a long time.

If you are on Minecraft PC in Creative mode, then you can build it super quickly using commands.

Use the Fill command to make a tall building like this:

1 **Start at a bottom corner of where you want your building to be and stand exactly where you want the bottom of your building to be.**

2 **Press F3 to record your coordinates.**

If you are on a Mac, press fn and then F3. A lot of information appears. Look for Block: and write down the three numbers after it. These numbers are the exact location in your world where you're standing.

3 **Move to the opposite corner and record your coordinates.**

4 **After you have written down where you are, move in the air to the opposite corner and record your coordinates there.**

5 Type in the Fill Command with the coordinates.

Type

```
/fill <Step 2 Numbers> <Step 3 Numbers>
```

```
/fill -537 4 1016 -529 26 1008_
```

6 Choose a material.

Type **minecraft:stone** if you want stone. If you don't know the exact name, type the first letter of the material and then tab to see your options.

```
minecraft:stone_pressure_plate, minecraft:standing_sign,
minecraft:structure_block, minecraft:structure_void,
minecraft:stone_slab2, minecraft:stone_button,
minecraft:stained_glass, minecraft:stone_slab,
minecraft:stained_glass_pane, minecraft:stone,
minecraft:standing_banner, minecraft:stained_hardened_clay,
minecraft:stone_brick_stairs, minecraft:sticky_piston,
minecraft:stonebrick, minecraft:stone_stairs
```

```
/fill -537 4 1016 -529 26 1008 minecraft:stone_pressure_plate
```

7 Add the material to your command.

To add stone, for example, type

```
/fill <Step 2 Numbers> <Step 3 Numbers>
   minecraft:stone
```

```
/fill -537 4 1016 -529 26 1008 minecraft:stone
```

8 **Type** 0 **and then** outline.

For example:

```
/fill <Step 2 Numbers> <Step 3 Numbers>
   minecraft:stone 0 outline
```

`/fill -537 4 1016 -529 26 1008 minecraft:stone 0 outline`

Tada! You made a really tall building!

834 blocks filled

If you open the door and you see this:

Then you probably want to make your building one block beneath where you stand. Don't worry! You can fix that!

 If you ever mess up, you can run the exact same command, but replace the material with air. Just type /, push the up key on your keyboard, move left, and place your materials with minecraft:air.

```
/fill -537 4 1016 -529 26 1008 minecraft:air 0 outline
```

After you have either broken all of the blocks or used the same command with `material:air`, you can rerun the command by pressing / on your keyboard and then pressing the up key. Make sure that you change the material back and that you change your first number to be one number lower.

```
/fill -537 3 1016 -529 26 1008 minecraft:stone 0 outline
```

After you make the changes to your building to make it one block lower, you should see this when you make a door:

And your building will look something like this:

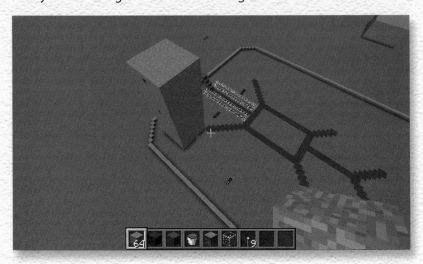

You can do this for all of your tall buildings, and then you can have lots of them really quickly, like this:

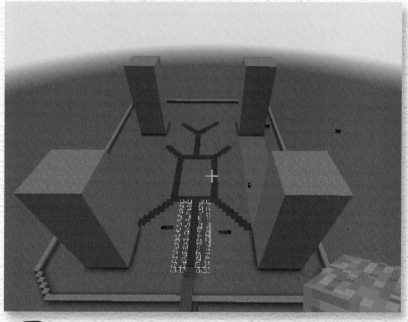

 To make these four buildings, the coordinates are

```
/fill -537 3 1016 -529 26 1008 ...
/fill -537 3 1044 -529 26 1052 ...
/fill -584 3 1044 -576 26 1052 ...
/fill -584 3 1016 -529 26 1008 ...
```

You might notice a lot of repeated numbers. This is good! The 3 and 26 are always the same because the buildings always are the same height. The other numbers are similar because they are lined up in a square, like you see in the preceding picture!

MAKING A MOAT

You can also make structures underground using the Fill command. For example, if you want to make a moat, you can replace grass blocks with water blocks around your wall, like this:

```
/fill -522 3 1067 -518 1 1032
    minecraft:water 0 replace
```

Your numbers will be different depending on where you are standing.

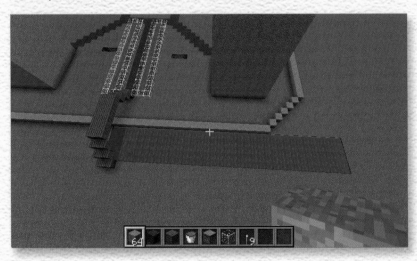

/fill -518 1 1028 -522 3 997 minecraft:water 0 replace_

When you run that command, you will get water.

And if you continue to dig out where the water goes, you can create an entire moat!

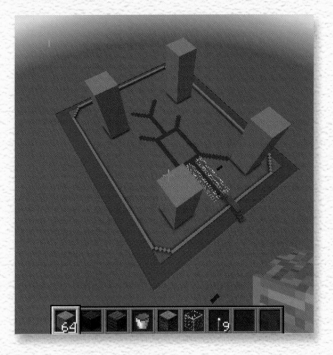

BUILDING A SIMPLE HOUSE

After you know how to use the Fill command to make large structures like skyscrapers and moats, you can copy and paste buildings that have more detail.

First, build a simple house, like this:

Then, just like you did for the fill command, find the coordinates for one corner of the building.

You can get the exact corner, or you can get a little extra so that space is around each house. To get extra, just stay a couple of blocks away from your building.

Then get the coordinates for the other corner of the building.

If you have a roof that is taller in the middle, make sure that you are all the way above the highest point of your building so that you don't accidentally cut it off.

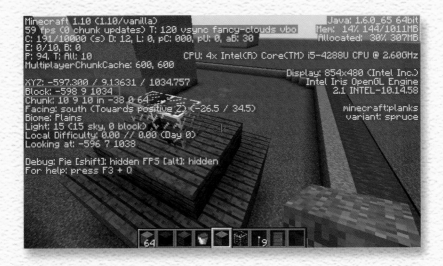

Then you can walk to where you want to put a clone of the building and type this command:

```
/clone <First Coordinate> <Second Coordinate>
    ~ ~ ~ replace normal
```

And you can do this however many times you want, creating a bunch of houses!

If you mess up, you can always use the Fill command with air to undo it.

Now your city is really starting to look like a city!

USING COMMANDS TO BUILD

After you know how to use the Fill and Clone commands, you can make a lot of things for your city really quickly.

You can review the two commands in the following sections.

FILL COMMAND

Using the Fill command is a really fast way to fill in a large area with a certain block type. You can make rectangles that are filled in or hollow, and you can even put walls around something you have already built in Minecraft. This makes building really fast and easy when you're on Minecraft PC. Here are some steps to follow to use the Fill command:

1 Find the coordinates for both corners of where you want to fill.

You can use the <F3> key to open up all the information about your Minecraft world. Look for the Block, and there you will find the three numbers that you need to record your coordinates. Make sure that you write them down!

2 Choose a material.

You can either look up the proper names of all Minecraft Blocks on a website with your parent's permission, or you can just start typing the name and type <TAB> to get a list of everything.

3 Type 0 to choose the first version of this material.

If there are different types of the same block (like colored wool or colored stained glass), you can put other numbers to get the different colors.

4 **Choose an option for filling.**

There are five options for filling:

» **replace:** Everything in the area will be replaced by the material you choose.

» **destroy:** Everything in the area will be destroyed. You can use this instead of doing the Fill command with air as the material.

» **keep:** Anything that is in the area will be kept, unless it is air, which is replaced with the material you choose.

» **hollow:** This will replace everything in the area with air, except the outside layer. This would be great for building a cave.

» **outline:** This will replace the outside layer with the material you choose, but will leave everything on the inside as it is already.

CLONE COMMAND

Using the Clone command makes copying Minecraft structures super fast. You can spend hours on one building and then use the Clone command to copy everything that you have done without having to spend hours on the second one. The Clone command is perfect for really big buildings or buildings that have a lot of details.

1 **Find the coordinates for both corners of what you want to clone.**

You can use the <F3> key to open up all the information about your Minecraft world. Look for the Block, and there you will find the three numbers that you need to record your coordinates. Make sure that you write them down!

2 **Move to where you want to put your cloned building and type ~ ~ ~.**

This key is the same as saying "My current location."

3 **Choose an option for cloning.**

There are three options for cloning:

» **replace:** The cloned building will replace anything that is in its way.

» **masked:** Only non-air blocks are cloned. If you have a hollow house, you can clone it over a bed, and the bed won't get replaced with air.

» **filtered:** This one is complicated, but you can add a list of blocks that will not be copied. For example, if you don't copy the glass blocks, air will be placed there instead.

4 **Choose another option for cloning.**

There are three more options for cloning:

» **normal:** If you want to do normal, you do not have to type it. It will do exactly what you think: Copy one building and place it where you're standing.

» **move:** This option will place the copied building, but it will remove the original. It's great if you just want to move an entire building over a few blocks.

» **force:** Sometimes you accidentally copy the building and place it inside of the same building. If you want to do this, you add force so that it will still place the copy, even though it is inside of the one you are trying to copy.

PLAYING AROUND WITH COMMANDS

Commands can be really tricky, but you should open up a new world that you can play around in and try them out. Build buildings, clone them, and fill them. Try all the different options. It can be challenging, but after you have commands working, you can really get your city growing quickly!

MAKING YOUR CITY UNIQUE

Finally, you can go around and add more details to your city. Make each building unique. Add more windows and furniture.

PROJECT 5 BUILDING CITY ATTRACTIONS

BUILDING A LOT OF BUILDINGS ALL AROUND YOUR CITY IS IMPORTANT, BUT YOU ALSO SHOULD BUILD ATTRACTIONS — THINGS FOR PEOPLE TO DO IN YOUR CITY. In this project, you learn how to make a lot of really neat attractions that you can put all over your city.

Your city will be a lot easier to build and look a lot better if you plan where your buildings and attractions will be first.

FANCY FOUNTAINS

You can build fountains in a lot of ways. In this section, you see how to build three different kinds of fountains.

Your fountains can have normal water in them, or you can put lava in your fountain to make it glow.

SIMPLE ONE-BLOCK FOUNTAIN

The simplest fountain is made with one block and one bucket of water.

1 **Place a block where you want your fountain to start.**

2 **Pour a bucket of water on top of the block.**

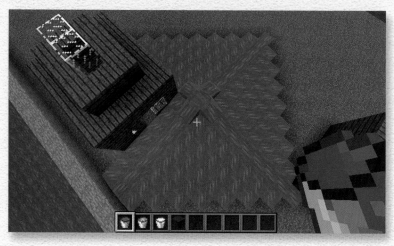

A simple one-block fountain is a great option for when you are playing in Survival mode because you don't need to gather a lot of resources for it. It's also very easy to do in Minecraft PE.

Even though you can easily build a one-block fountain, the water will go everywhere. An easy fix if you are in Creative mode is to add a barrier around your fountain.

Another easy fix is to break the blocks below your single block so that the water has somewhere to go.

And building a tall fountain is easy in Minecraft PE or Survival mode, too.

TALL FOUNTAINS

You can make one-block fountains a little more interesting by making them taller.

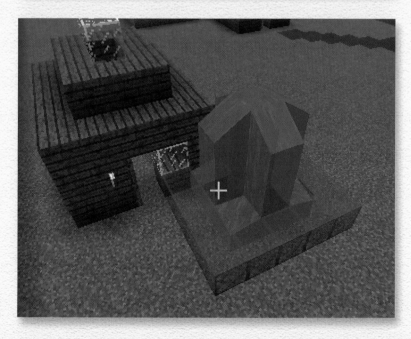

You can do the digging trick with taller fountains, too.

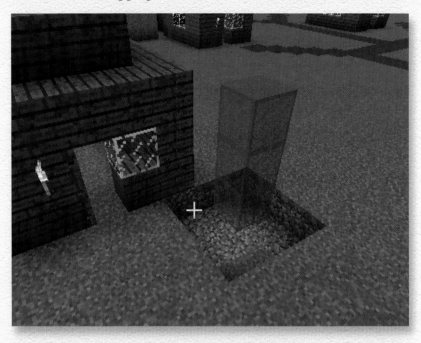

You can also do it on Minecraft PE.

And don't forget, you can always have it be lava instead of water.

 If you have water and lava near each other, they will turn into stone, cobblestone, or obsidian if they touch.

TALL FOUNTAINS WITHOUT WALLS

A really fun way to build fountains is to build them up high and let them just fall to the ground.

1 Build a really tall tower.

2 Dig three blocks below the tower.

3 Break all the blocks except the top one.

4 Pour water on the top block and quickly break the top block.

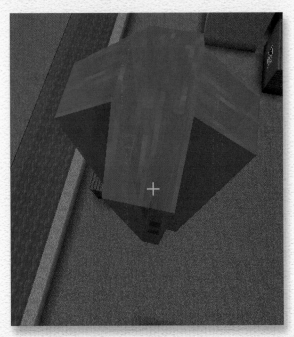

5 Watch the water flow.

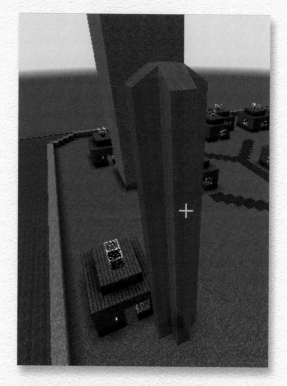

WIDE FOUNTAINS WITHOUT WALLS

Fountains can be tall, but they can also be wide.

1 Dig a long hole (trench) and put a single block up high above the trench.

2 Pour water (or lava) on top of the block and immediately break it.

3 Put another block above the trench, but a little lower.

4 Pour water (or lava) on top of the second block and immediately break it.

Watch as your fountain flows.

 Dealing with tall and wide fountains can be tricky, and it is really easy for your water or lava to get out of hand. Don't worry if you mess up. You can always rebuild.

If you want to stop your fountain water or lava from flowing, just put a block where your water or lava stream starts. The block will cut off the supply and make all the water and lava disappear.

You can always go to another area of your world and practice making fountains before making them in your city.

WATER SLIDES

What can be more fun on a summer day than going down a huge water slide? Nothing!

Building a water slide is not very hard. All you have to do is build a tall bridge and then fill it with water.

1 Build a bridge with walls on the side.

Your bridge should have steps going up to the top, and steps coming down. It should be at least three blocks wide so that there is a wall on each side and you can slide down the middle.

2 Put a block in the middle at the top of your bridge.

The block will prevent the water from going down the stairs.
You need to be able to walk up to the top of the slide.

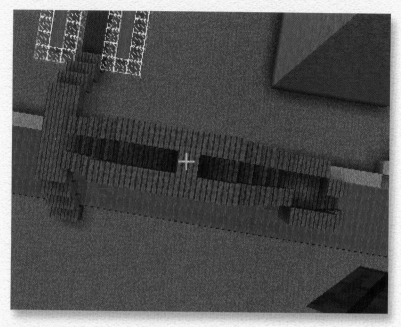

3 Put water on the slide side.

You may have to add some extra water if your slide is very
wide or tall.

4 Slide down.

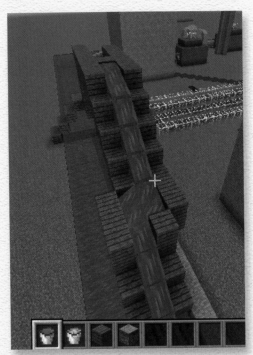

If you pour more than one bucket of water, then the flow of water may get messed up. You can see the lines in the water that tell you which direction the water is flowing. You want all your water to be flowing like this:

But it might accidentally become like this:

which will make you just sit still when you get to this part because the water pushes you into the corner!

MULTIPLE STORY BUILDINGS

In Project 4, you learn how to build really tall buildings, like these:

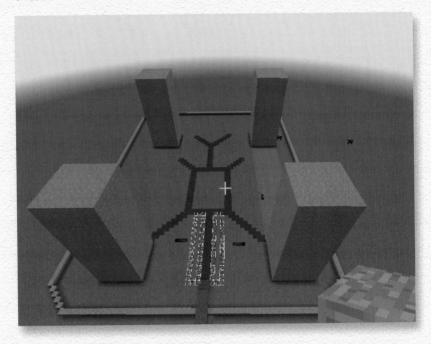

Really tall buildings are not that interesting unless you can explore them. Don't worry; you can quickly make a few different stories in these tall buildings.

1 **Put a wooden staircase, wooden plank block, and torch in your inventory.**

Leave a stone block in your inventory, too, so that you can replace any stone blocks that you accidentally break.

2 Make a doorway and add a door to your building.

Changing to clear weather

3 Place a wooden staircase where you want your wrap-around staircase to start.

4 Point your mouse to the bottom-left corner of the next block on the wall above your first staircase and place the second staircase there.

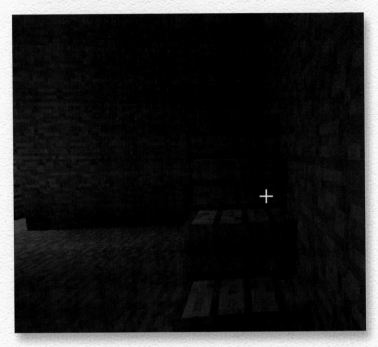

5 Keep moving along the wall until you have a staircase all the way to the top of the building.

Put torches along the way so that you can see.

6 **Pick where you want each story to be and place the wooden blocks across the entire building to make the floor.**

Make sure that you leave room to go up and down the stairs.

7 When you are at the top story, break one of the blocks in the ceiling and put stairs going up to the roof.

ROLLER COASTERS

A roller coaster in Minecraft is basically a big staircase with a rail on it.

RAIL TYPES

You will use two types of rails in this section:

» **Powered rail:** When you put a redstone torch next to them, they light up and push the minecart that is on them. These are great for the start of your roller coaster or when you need the roller coaster to go on flat ground or uphill!

» **Rail:** When you use a regular rail, the minecart will move if it is going downhill or you are in it and are pushing it forward. These rails are great for downhill tracks and the end of your roller coaster, when you want your minecart to slow down.

THE STRUCTURE

First, you will need to build the track where you want your roller coaster to be. You should start somewhere high so that your minecart can pick up speed.

And you can make some fun designs with your roller coaster — for example, this one goes through the next building.

And the exit leads you to your house!

THE TRACK

After you have built your roller coaster structure, you can add the track.

1 Start by putting a redstone torch at the top of your structure.

2 Then add the powered rail, making sure that it's lit up by the redstone torch.

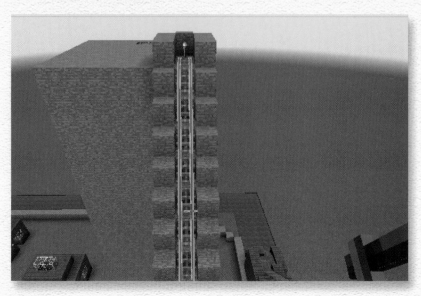

3 Then add the regular rail.

4 Finally, put a minecart at the top, left-click to get in, and move forward to start your ride.

MAKING YOUR CITY UNIQUE

The most important thing to remember when you are a Minecraft City Architect is that the city can be anything you want it to be! You can have roller coasters that lead into water slides that go underground.

You can plant farms and flowers and have cows and pigs and horses running around everywhere.

You can even have 100 houses that all look the same and have enough room for every single one of your friends to join in.

This is your world. Make sure that you have fun and don't worry if you mess up. Minecraft worlds are huge, and you can always build another one.

ABOUT THE AUTHOR

Sarah Guthals received her PhD from University of California, San Diego, in Computer Science, specializing in Computer Science Education in 2014. During graduate school, she built the beta version of CodeSpells, a 3D immersive video game designed to teach children to code through playing a wizard and writing spells.

Sarah went on to cofound ThoughtSTEM, a company that builds software (for example, LearnToMod), curriculum, and pedagogies for teaching children to code and empowering K–12 teachers to teach their students. She has written two books around modding Minecraft, launched a Coursera course for teachers interested in teaching coding, and was recently named Forbes 30 under 30 in Science.

Sarah's passion is making coding accessible to everyone, with the goal of making it a basic literacy.

DEDICATION

I would like to dedicate this book to my close friends and families who have supported me, not only in writing this book, but in becoming who I am today. I'd like to specifically dedicate this book to Adrian Guthals, who has always helped me to see that, with passion and dedication, I can really do anything I want.

AUTHOR'S ACKNOWLEDGMENTS

I would like to acknowledge all of the hard work that went into making Minecraft an incredibly fun and open game played by millions around the world. I would also like to acknowledge the teachers and parents around the world who have recognized the importance of a game like Minecraft in teaching so many valuable lessons to our next generation of builders.

PUBLISHER'S ACKNOWLEDGMENTS

Senior Acquisitions Editor: Amy Fandrei

Production Editor: Tamilmani Varadharaj

Project Editor: Kelly Ewing

Copy Editor: Kelly Ewing

Editorial Assistant: Serena Novosel

Sr. Editorial Assistant: Cherie Case

Reviewer: Paige Ewing